ANiMALS
AND THEIR
BABIES

DOGS
AND PUPPIES

By Annabelle Lynch

Contents

W
FRANKLIN WATTS
LONDON•SYDNEY

GROWING INSIDE

This dog has babies growing in her **tummy.**

The dog's tummy gets bigger and bigger as her puppies grow!

After about 60 days, the puppies are ready to be born.

3

GIVING BIRTH

A mother dog finds somewhere safe and warm to have her **babies.**

The mother dog licks her
newborn puppies clean.
She stays close to keep
them **warm**.

Snuggle up!

SEEING
AND HEARING

When they are born, puppies cannot see or hear. Their eyes and ears stay closed.

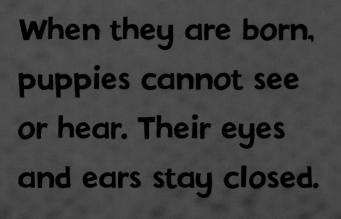

Puppies begin to **see** and **hear** when they are about two weeks old.

Puppies stay close together so they are **safe**.

FEEDING

Puppies can
smell as soon
as they are born.
This helps them to
find their mother's milk.

Puppies suck the milk out of their mother's **teats.**

They feed only on their mother's milk until they are about **four weeks** old.

MOVING

Puppies learn to walk when they are about three weeks old.

They are a bit **wobbly** at first!

Now puppies can move
around, they love to find out
more about the world.

Sometimes they get a bit tired though!

GROWING TEETH

When they are two or three weeks old, puppies start growing their first teeth. These teeth are small but very **sharp!**

Now puppies can start eating solid food. They still drink their mother's milk, but they can drink water now too.

Crunch!

Munch!

KEEPING CLEAN

Puppies are covered in **soft** fur.

While puppies are still young, their mother licks them to keep them clean. This is called grooming.

Slurp!

As they grow
up, puppies
learn how to
clean
themselves.

PLAY AND LEARN

Puppies love to **play!** Playing keeps them healthy and helps them learn how to run, chase, jump, catch and even fight.

Playing also teaches puppies about the world around them.

Splash!

Brrrr!

As they grow up, puppies can look
after themselves better. At around two or three
months old, pet puppies are ready to leave
their mother and go to a **new home**.

Puppies keep
growing and changing
until they are about
a year old. At
six months old,
they get a new,
adult coat of fur.

A GROWN-UP DOG

By the time they reach their first birthday, almost all puppies are fully grown.

They are now called dogs.

Grown-up dogs can have puppies of their own.
They still love to **play** though!

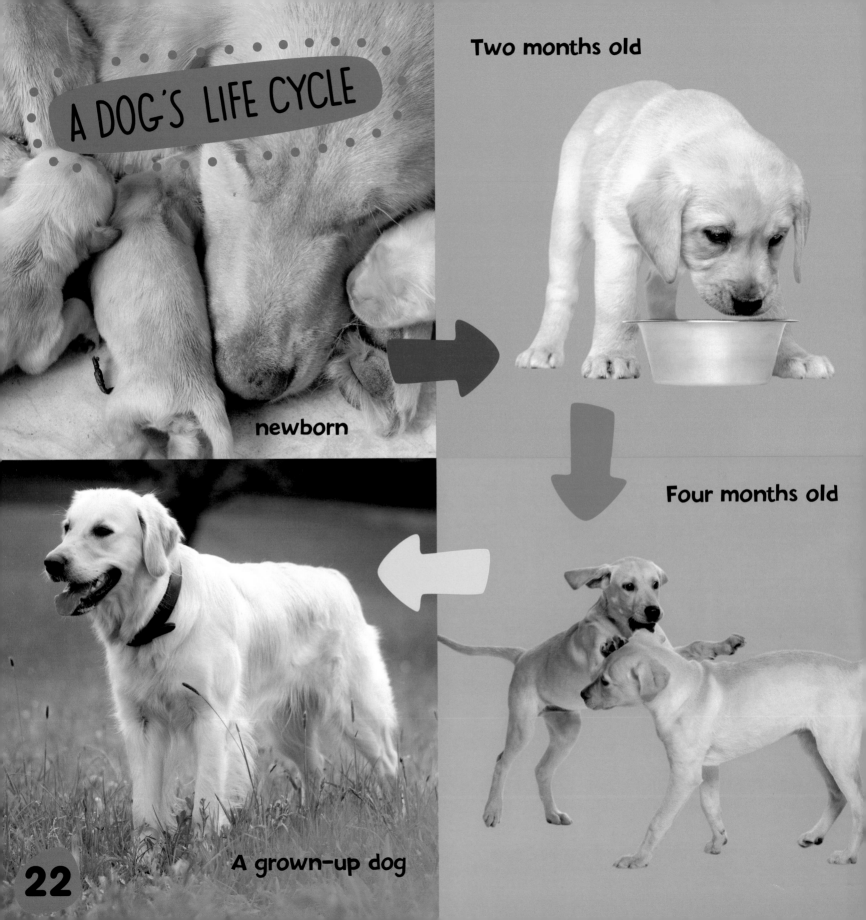

A DOG'S LIFE CYCLE

newborn

Two months old

Four months old

A grown-up dog

fur

grooming

WORD BANK

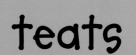

solid food

newborn

teats

INDEX

Franklin Watts
Published in paperback in Great Britain in 2019
by The Watts Publishing Group

Copyright © The Watts Publishing Group 2016

Series Editor: Julia Bird
Series Designer: Basement 68

Picture credits: Nancy Dressel/Dreamstime: 14–15, 23tr.
Robert Fesus/Shutterstock: 1tr, 13, 23cr. Fnsy/Shutterstock:
8–9. Carson Ganci/Alamy: 18. Vaness Grossemy/Alamy:
front cover. Simon Hart/Alamy: 4–5, 24. Eric Isselee/
Shutterstock: 19, 22tr, 22br, 23tl. Rita Kochmarjova/
Shutterstock: 21. Sergey Lavrentev/Dreamstime: 6, 23cl.
Life on white/Alamy: 1bl, 10, 11. limitedqstock/Alamy: 17.
Luffmorgan/Dreamstime: 16. Marina Olena/Shutterstock:
7. Harry Page/Alamy: 2–3, 23b. Susan Smitz/Shutterstock:
12, 20. stockphoto mania/Shutterstock: 22tl. Umkehrer/
Shutterstock: 22bl.

Every attempt has been made to clear copyright.
Should there be any inadvertent omission please
apply to the publisher for rectification.

ISBN 978 1 4451 4837 3

Printed in China

MIX
Paper from
responsible sources
FSC® C104740
FSC
www.fsc.org

Franklin Watts
An imprint of
Hachette Children's Group
Part of The Watts Publishing Group
Carmelite House
50 Victoria Embankment
London EC4Y 0DZ

An Hachette UK Company
www.hachette.co.uk

www.franklinwatts.co.uk